MW01171910

Music Literacy 7

Sarah Stopher

Copyright © 2018 Sarah Stopher
All rights reserved.

No part of this book may be reproduced in any form or by any electronic or mechanical means including information storage and retrieval systems, without permission in writing from the author.

ISBN-13: 9781975643119

Printed in the United States of America
First Printing: December 2018

Cover image © Roberto Giovannini | Dreamstime.com

www.stophermusic.com

Contents

Section 1: Aural

Rhythmic Dictation (16 marks)

Add the stems and beams to the pitch provided using the following elements:

Pitch Dictation (12 marks)

Notate each melody using the rhythm provided and the pitches on the right.

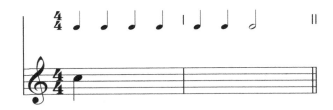

Melodic Dictation (16 marks)

Notate these melodies using the pitches provided and these rhythmic elements:

Interval Identification (4 marks)

The first note is given for you. Write in the missing note and then name the intervals from the following:
Tone, Semitone, Perfect 5th or Perfect 8ve

1. _____   2. _____

Chord Identifcation (4 marks)

Identify these chords as major or minor. Each chord will be played twice.

1._____   2. _____   3. _____   4. _____

TOTAL MARKS   /52   CONVERTED   %

Rhythmic Dictation (16 marks)

Add the stems and beams to the pitch provided using the following elements:

Pitch Dictation (12 marks)

Notate each melody using the rhythm provided and the pitches on the right.

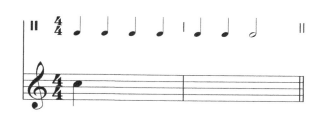

Melodic Dictation (16 marks)

Notate these melodies using the pitches provided and the following rhythmic elements:

Interval Identification (4 marks)

The first note is given for you. Write in the missing note and then name the intervals from the following:
Tone, Semitone, Perfect 5th or Perfect 8ve

1. _____

2. _____

Chord Identifcation (4 marks)

Identify these chords as major or minor. Each chord will be played twice.

1._____   2. _____   3. _____   4. _____

TOTAL MARKS   **/52**   **CONVERTED**   **%**

Rhythmic Dictation (16 marks)

Add the stems and beams to the pitch provided using the following elements:

Pitch Dictation (12 marks)

Notate each melody using the rhythm provided and the pitches on the right.

Melodic Dictation (20 marks)

Notate these melodies using the pitches provided and the following rhythmic elements:

Interval Identification (4 marks)

The first note is given for you. Write in the missing note and then name the intervals from the following:
Tone, Semitone, Perfect 5th or Perfect 8ve

1. _____   2. _____

Chord Identifcation (4 marks)

Identify these chords as major or minor. Each chord will be played twice.

1._____   2. _____   3. _____   4. _____

TOTAL MARKS   **/56**   **CONVERTED**   **%**

Rhythmic Dictation (16 marks)

Add the stems and beams to the pitch provided using the following elements:

Pitch Dictation (12 marks)

Notate each melody using the rhythm provided and the pitches on the right.

Melodic Dictation (18 marks)

Notate these melodies using the pitches provided and the following
rhythmic elements:

Interval Identification (4 marks)

The first note is given for you. Write in the missing note and then name the intervals from the following:
Tone, Semitone, Perfect 5th or Perfect 8ve

1. _____

2. _____

Chord Identifcation (4 marks)

Identify these chords as major or minor. Each chord will be played twice.

1._____   2. _____   3. _____   4. _____

TOTAL MARKS   **/54**   **CONVERTED**   **%**

Rhythmic Dictation (16 marks)

Add the stems and beams to the pitch provided using the following elements:

Pitch Dictation (12 marks)

Notate each melody using the rhythm provided and the pitches on the right.

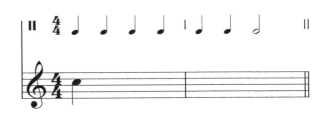

Melodic Dictation (22 marks)

Notate these melodies using the pitches provided and the following rhythmic elements:

Interval Identification (4 marks)

The first note is given for you. Write in the missing note and then name the intervals from the following: Tone, Semitone, Perfect 5th or Perfect 8ve

1. _____

2. _____

Chord Identifcation (4 marks)

Identify these chords as major or minor. Each chord will be played twice.

1._____   2. _____   3. _____   4. _____

TOTAL MARKS   /58   CONVERTED   %

Rhythmic Dictation (16 marks)

Add the stems and beams to the pitch provided using the following elements:

Pitch Dictation (15 marks)

Notate each melody using the rhythm provided and the pitches on the right.

Melodic Dictation (12 marks)

Notate these melodies using the pitches provided and the following rhythmic elements:

Interval Identification (4 marks)

The first note is given for you. Write in the missing note and then name the intervals from the following: Tone, Semitone, Perfect 5th or Perfect 8ve

1. _____   2. _____

Chord Identifcation (4 marks)

Identify these chords as major or minor. Each chord will be played twice.

1._____   2. _____   3. _____   4. _____

TOTAL MARKS   /51   CONVERTED   %

Rhythmic Dictation (16 marks)

Add the stems and beams to the pitch provided using the following elements:

Pitch Dictation (16 marks)

Notate each melody using the rhythm provided and the pitches on the right.

Melodic Dictation (11 marks)

Notate these melodies using the pitches provided and the following rhythmic elements:

Interval Identification (4 marks)

The first note is given for you. Write in the missing note and then name the intervals from the following: Tone, Semitone, Perfect 5th or Perfect 8ve

1. _____

2. _____

Chord Identifcation (4 marks)

Identify these chords as major or minor. Each chord will be played twice.

1._____   2. _____   3. _____   4. _____

TOTAL MARKS   **/51**   **CONVERTED**   **%**

Rhythmic Dictation (16 marks)

Add the stems and beams to the pitch provided using the following elements:

Pitch Dictation (16 marks)

Notate each melody using the rhythm provided and the pitches on the right.

Melodic Dictation (11 marks)

Notate these melodies using the pitches provided and the following rhythmic elements:

Interval Identification (4 marks)

The first note is given for you. Write in the missing note and then name the intervals from the following: Tone, Semitone, Perfect 5th or Perfect 8ve

1. _____

2. _____

Chord Identifcation (4 marks)

Identify these chords as major or minor. Each chord will be played twice.

1._____ 2. _____ 3. _____ 4. _____

TOTAL MARKS **/51** **CONVERTED** **%**

Rhythmic Dictation (16 marks)

Add the stems and beams to the pitch provided using the following elements:

Pitch Dictation (18 marks)

Notate each melody using the rhythm provided and the pitches on the right.

Melodic Dictation (14 marks)

Notate these melodies using the pitches provided and the following rhythmic elements:

Interval Identification (4 marks)

The first note is given for you. Write in the missing note and then name the intervals from the following: Tone, Semitone, Perfect 5th or Perfect 8ve

1. _____

2. _____

Chord Identifcation (4 marks)

Identify these chords as major or minor. Each chord will be played twice.

1._____   2. _____   3. _____   4. _____

TOTAL MARKS   **/56**   **CONVERTED**   **%**

Rhythmic Dictation (16 marks)

Add the stems and beams to the pitch provided using the following elements:

Pitch Dictation (16 marks)

Notate each melody using the rhythm provided and the pitches on the right.

Melodic Dictation (14 marks)

Notate these melodies using the pitches provided and the following rhythmic elements:

Interval Identification (4 marks)

The first note is given for you. Write in the missing note and then name the intervals from the following:
Tone, Semitone, Perfect 5th or Perfect 8ve

1. _____   2. _____

Chord Identifcation (4 marks)

Identify these chords as major or minor. Each chord will be played twice.

1._____   2. _____   3. _____   4. _____

TOTAL MARKS   **/54**   **CONVERTED**   **%**

Rhythmic Dictation (16 marks)

Add the stems and beams to the pitch provided using the following elements: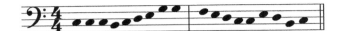

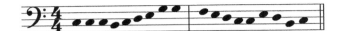 

Pitch Dictation (16 marks)

Notate each melody using the rhythm provided and the pitches on the right.

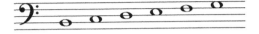

Melodic Dictation (15 marks)

Notate these melodies using the pitches provided and the following rhythmic elements:

Interval Identification (4 marks)

Add the missing note in the melody (the rhythm is above) and identify the interval under the brackets.

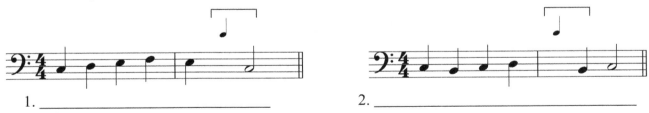

1. _____   2. _____

Chord Progression (8 marks)

Identify the chords in these progressions using I and V. Chord I will be played before the progression starts.

TOTAL MARKS   /59   CONVERTED   %

Rhythmic Dictation (16 marks)

Add the stems and beams to the pitch provided using the following elements:

Pitch Dictation (17 marks)

Notate each melody using the rhythm provided and the pitches on the right.

Melodic Dictation (15 marks)

Notate these melodies using the pitches provided and the following rhythmic elements:

Interval Identification (4 marks)

Add the missing note in the melody and identify the interval.

1. _____

2.

Chord Progression (8 marks)

Identify the chords in these progressions using I and IV. Chord I will be played before the progression starts.

TOTAL MARKS   **/60**   **CONVERTED**   **%**

Rhythmic Dictation (16 marks)

Add the stems and beams to the pitch provided using the following elements:

Pitch Dictation (16 marks)

Notate each melody using the rhythm provided and the pitches on the right.

Melodic Dictation (14 marks)

Notate these melodies using the pitches provided and the following rhythmic elements:

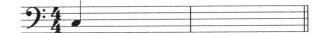

Interval Identification (4 marks)

Add the missing note in the melody and identify the interval.

1. _____

2. _____

Chord Progression (8 marks)

Identify the chords in these progressions using I and V. Chord I will be played before the progression starts.

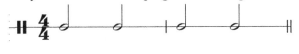

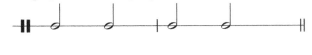

TOTAL MARKS   /58   **CONVERTED**   %

Rhythmic Dictation (16 marks)

Add the stems and beams to the pitch provided using the following elements:

Pitch Dictation (16 marks)

Notate each melody using the rhythm provided and the pitches on the right.

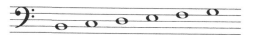

Melodic Dictation (16 marks)

Notate these melodies using the pitches provided and the following rhythmic elements: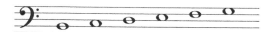

Interval Identification (4 marks)

Add the missing note in the melody and identify the interval.

1. _____

2. _____

Chord Progression (8 marks)

Identify the chords in these progressions using I and IV. Chord I will be played before the progression starts.

___ ___ ___ ___   ___ ___ ___ ___

TOTAL MARKS   **/60**   **CONVERTED**   **%**

Rhythmic Dictation (16 marks)

Add the stems and beams to the pitch provided using the following elements:

Pitch Dictation (16 marks)

Notate each melody using the rhythm provided and the pitches on the right.

Melodic Dictation (15 marks)

Notate these melodies using the pitches provided and the following rhythmic elements:

Interval Identification (4 marks)

Add the missing note in the melody and identify the interval.

1. _____   2. _____

Chord Progression (8 marks)

Identify the chords in these progressions using I and IV. Chord I will be played before the progression starts.

20   **TOTAL MARKS**   **/59**   **CONVERTED**   **%**

Rhythmic Dictation (16 marks)

Add the stems and beams to the pitch provided. There are no new rhythmic elements.

Pitch Dictation (17 marks)

Notate each melody using the rhythm provided.

Melodic Dictation (12 marks)

Notate these melodies. The first note (including rhythm) is given for you.

Interval Identification (4 marks)

Write in the missing note in this melody and then name the interval under the brackets.

1. _____   2. _____

Chord Progression (8 marks)

Identify the chords in these progressions using I, IV and V. Chord I will be played before the progression starts.

TOTAL MARKS   **/57**   **CONVERTED**   **%**

Rhythmic Dictation (16 marks)

Add the stems and beams to the pitch provided. There are no new rhythmic elements.

Pitch Dictation (17 marks)

Notate each melody using the rhythm provided.

Melodic Dictation (14 marks)

Notate these melodies. The first note (including rhythm) is given for you.

Interval Identification (4 marks)

Write in the missing note in this melody and then name the interval under the brackets.

1. _____   2. _____

Chord Progression (8 marks)

Identify the chords in these progressions using I, IV and V. Chord I will be played before the progression starts.

22 **TOTAL MARKS** /59 **CONVERTED** %

Rhythmic Dictation (16 marks)

Add the stems and beams to the pitch provided. There are no new rhythmic elements.

Pitch Dictation (15 marks)

Notate each melody using the rhythm provided.

Melodic Dictation (16 marks)

Notate these melodies. The first note (including rhythm) is given for you.

Interval Identification (4 marks)

Write in the missing note in this melody and then name the interval under the brackets.

1. _____   2. _____

Chord Progression (8 marks)

Identify the chords in these progressions using I, IV and V. Chord I will be played before the progression starts.

TOTAL MARKS   **/59**   **CONVERTED**   **%**

Rhythmic Dictation (16 marks)

Add the stems and beams to the pitch provided. There are no new rhythmic elements.

Pitch Dictation (18 marks)

Notate each melody using the rhythm provided.

Melodic Dictation (14 marks)

Notate these melodies. The first note (including rhythm) is given for you.

Interval Identification (4 marks)

Write in the missing note in this melody and then name the interval under the brackets.

1. _____

2. _____

Chord Progression (8 marks)

Identify the chords in these progressions using I, IV and V. Chord I will be played before the progression starts.

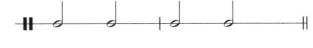

24   **TOTAL MARKS**   **/60**   **CONVERTED**   **%**

Rhythmic Dictation (16 marks)

Add the stems and beams to the pitch provided. There are no new rhythmic elements.

Pitch Dictation (16 marks)

Notate each melody using the rhythm provided.

Melodic Dictation (16 marks)

Notate these melodies. The first note (including rhythm) is given for you.

Interval Identification (4 marks)

Write in the missing note in this melody and then name the interval under the brackets.

1. _____   2. _____

Chord Progression (8 marks)

Identify the chords in these progressions using I, IV and V. Chord I will be played before the progression starts.

TOTAL MARKS   **/60**   **CONVERTED**   **%**

Section 2: Theory Lessons

Review: Notes in the Treble Clef

The treble clef is what we use for notes that are usually above middle C on the piano. There is a simple saying to help remember the names of these notes.

Pratice writing the treble clef.

Notes on the LINES: **E**very **G**ood **B**oy **D**eserves **F**ruit

Notes in the SPACES spell out **FACE**

Name these notes using CAPITAL letters.

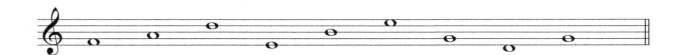

Write a treble clef at the start of each line and then write the notes using semibreves.

A	D	E	B	F	C	G

E	G	A	C	D	B	F

Review: Notes in the Bass Clef

The bass clef is what we use for notes that are usually below middle C on the piano. There is a simple saying to help remember the names of these notes.

Pratice writing the bass clef - be careful where you write the two dots.

Notes on the LINES: **G**reat **B**ig **D**reams **F**or **A**ustralia

Notes in the SPACES: **A**ll **C**ows **E**at **G**rass

Name these notes using CAPITAL letters.

Write a bass clef at the start of each line and then write the notes using semibreves.

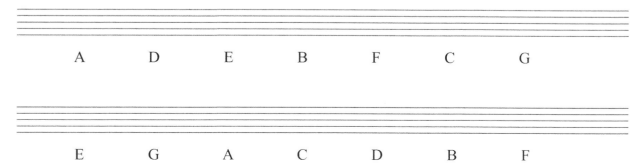

Review: Note Values (and their rests)

Each time you add something to a note (like a stem or colour fill) the note values halves.

Complete the details for each note below.

Note	Name	Value	Rest
𝅝	Semibreve	4 beats	▬
𝅗𝅥	_____	_____	▬
𝅘𝅥	_____	_____	𝄽
𝅘𝅥𝅮	_____	_____	𝄾
𝅘𝅥𝅯	_____	_____	𝄿

Major and Pentatonic Scales

Major - based on C to C on the piano using only white notes.

When you change the starting note, you need to add either sharps or flats.

Key signature: 1 sharp, ___ sharp   Scale: _____

Key signature: 1 flat, ___ flat   Scale: _____

Pentatonic

The major pentatonic scale uses notes 1, 2, 3, 5 and 6 of the major scale.
Always add number 1 at the top.

Key Signatures

What is the order of sharps in key signatures? _____
Write them correctly on the stave.

What is the order of flats in key signatures? _____
Write them correctly on the stave.

There are several ways to remember how many sharps or flats are in a major key. One of the simplest is by using the circle of 5ths. For each key to the right around the circle, you add a sharp. For each key to the left, you add a flat.

At this stage, you only need to know the key signatures up to 1 sharp and 1 flat.

What are these keys? Fill in the major keys.

MAJOR: _____   _____   _____

     No sharps or flats   1 sharp   1 flat

Below is the circle of 5ths up to 4 sharps and 4 flats. Label the major keys and write in the tonic note. C major is done for you - count up five notes for right side (sharps), and down five notes for the left side (flats).

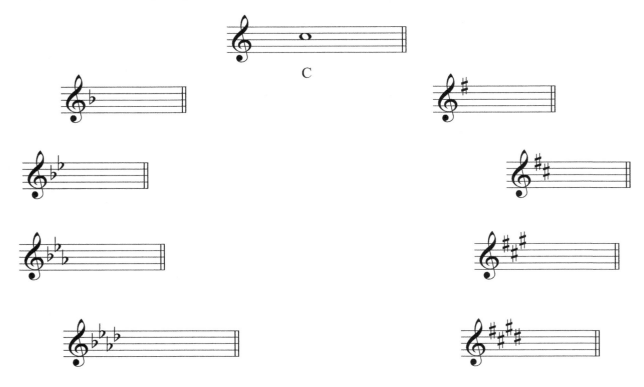

C

Writing Key Signatures

When using the bass clef, the key signatures are all written 1 line or space lower as shown below.

G major

F major

Practice writing the key signature of G major in the treble clef.
1. Write the clef
2. Write the sharp on the correct line
3. Finish with a double bar line

Practice writing the key signature of G major in the bass clef using the same process.

Practice writing the key signature of F major in the treble clef using the same process.

Practice writing the key signature of F major in the bass clef using the same process.

Scale Practice

Write the scales according to the directions given.

C major in the bass clef using semibreves

F major in the treble clef with a key signature using semibreves

G major in the bass clef with a key signature using semibreves

F major in the bass clef with accidentals using semibreves

G major in the treble clef with accidentals using semibreves

Pentatonic starting on C using semibreves in the treble clef

Pentatonic starting on F using semibreves in the bass celf

Scale Degree Names

Identify the name of each scale degree in the major scale and write down a hint to help you remember each of them.

Scale Degree Name   Hint

1 _____   _____

2 _____   _____

3 _____   _____

4 _____   _____

5 _____   _____

6 _____   _____

7 _____   _____

8 _____   _____

Simple Time Signatures

Simple time signatures have beats that are subdivided into groups of 2.
For example, a crotchet is divided into 2 quavers.

2/4 Simple Duple: 2 crotchet beats in a bar

3/4 Simple Triple: 3 crotchet beats in a bar

4/4 Simple Quadruple: 4 crotchet beats in a bar

Compound Time Signatures

Compound time signatures have beats that are subdivided into groups of 3.
For example, a dotted crotchet is divided into 3 quavers.

6/8 Compound Duple: 2 ♩. beats in a bar
           6 ♪ pulses

Add time signatures to these melodies.

Rhythmic Subdivision in Simple Time

What are the different subdivisions of the crotchet beat in simple time?
Write them in the space below.

Important Rule for $\frac{4}{4}$ time:

You can't have four quavers grouped together over the middle of the bar. You must be able to divide the bar in half.

Rewrite these excerpts with the correct note grouping.

Rhythmic Subdivision in Compound Time

What are the different subdivisions of the dotted crotchet beat in compound time?
Write them in the space below?

Rewrite these excerpts with the correct note grouping.

Major and Minor Intervals

What does the word 'interval' refer to in music? _____

Major intervals are based on the major scale.

For example, from C to D is a *major 2nd.*

Major 2nd

Intervals of a 4th, 5th and 8ve are known as *perfect* intervals

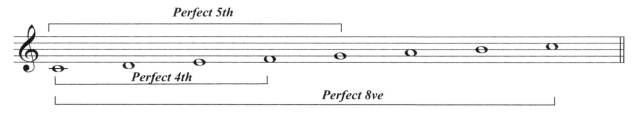

Perfect 5th

Perfect 4th

Perfect 8ve

Identify these intervals as either: Major 2nd, Perfect 4th, Perfect 5th or Perfect 8ve.

_____

Minor intervals are a semitone smaller than the major interval. A minor 2nd is only a semitone.

Major 2nd   *Minor 2nd*

Identify these intervals as either: Minor 2nd or Major 2nd

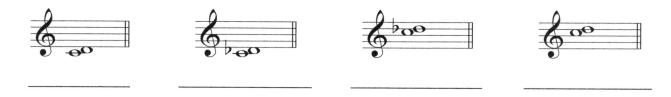

_____   _____   _____   _____

Interval Recognition - Treble Clef

Identify these intervals as either: Minor 2nd, Major 2nd, Perfect 4th, Perfect 5th or Perfect 8ve.

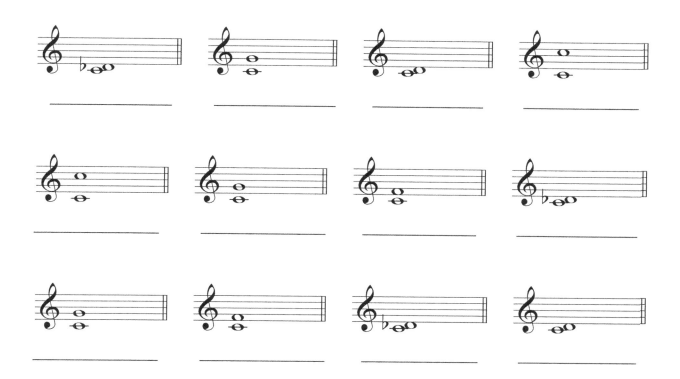

Write the intervals as indicated above the given note.

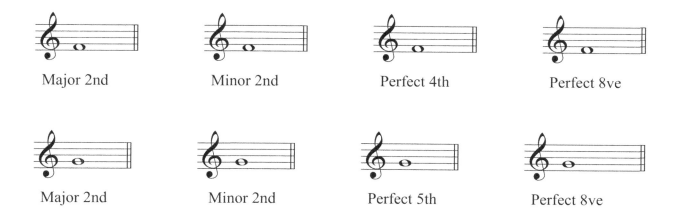

Interval Recognition - Bass Clef

Identify these intervals as either: Minor 2nd, Major 2nd, Perfect 4th, Perfect 5th or Perfect 8ve.

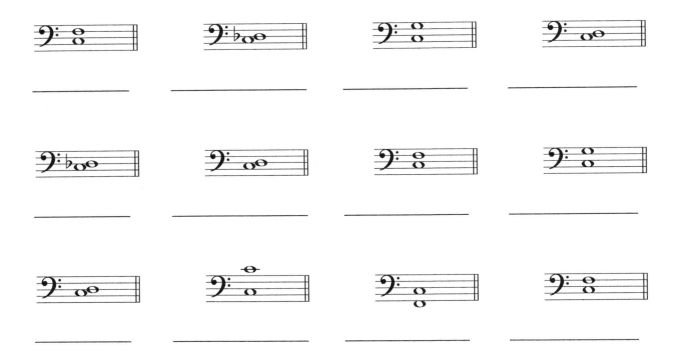

Write the intervals as indicated above the given note.

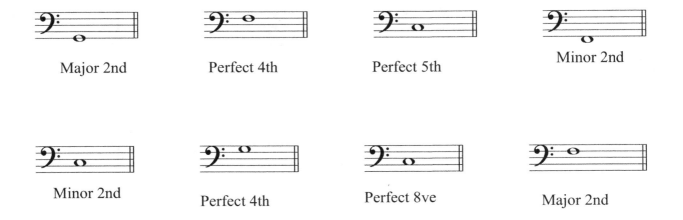

Major 2nd

Perfect 4th

Perfect 5th

Minor 2nd

Minor 2nd

Perfect 4th

Perfect 8ve

Major 2nd

Intervals

Intervals can be identified aurally or visually. For each interval, there are many songs you can choose to help you remember what they sound like.

Minor 2nd

Song: _____

Major 2nd

Song: _____

Minor 3rd

Song: _____

Major 3rd

Song: _____

Perfect 4th

Song: _____

Perfect 5th

Song: _____

Perfect 8ve

Song: _____

Triads

Triads are made up of a 3 notes - all on lines, or all on spaces.
They should be equally spread out as shown here:

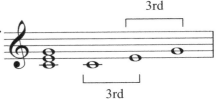

Write a triad above the following notes:

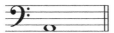  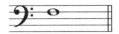

 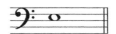 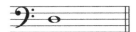

Primary Triads

Primary triads are bulit on the tonic, subdominant and dominant scale degrees and are labelled with Roman numerals.

What scale degrees are these?

Tonic _____   Subdominant _____   Dominant _____

Now write these as Roman numerals.

Tonic _____   Subdominant _____   Dominant _____

Label the scale degree numbers for the C major scale below (using normal numbers)

For each of these scales, write the primary triads in the manuscript below. Remember to add the correct clef, key signature and end with a double bar line.

C major - treble clef

C major - bass clef

F major - treble clef

F major - bass clef

G major - treble clef

G major - bass clef

Section 3: Theory Practice

Theory - skills practice 1

Note review: Treble clef

Write the C major scale in the treble clef (use semibreves and remember the double bar line)

Write the C major pentatonic scale in the bass clef

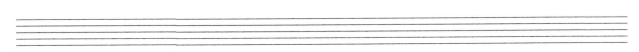

Name these key signatures and write the tonic.

_____   _____   _____

Write these intervals above the written note

Minor 2nd   Perfect 5th   Perfect 4th

Write a triad above each note.

  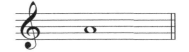

Insert a time signature for this piece. What is the metre? _____

Theory - skills practice 2

Note review: Bass clef

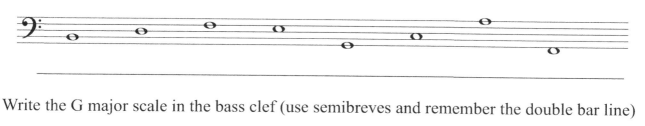

Write the G major scale in the bass clef (use semibreves and remember the double bar line)

Write the G major pentatonic scale in the treble clef

Write the key signatures for the tonic provided.

  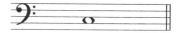

Identify these intervals from the following options:minor 2nd, major 2nd, perfect 4th, perfect 5th, perfect 8ve

 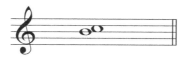 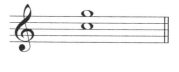

Write a triad above each note.

  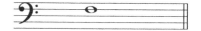

Rewrite these bars with the correct note grouping.

Theory - skills practice 3

Note review: Treble clef - write these notes using semibreves.

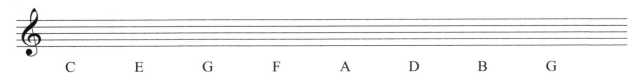

     C   E   G   F   A   D   B   G

Write the F major scale in the treble clef (use semibreves and remember the double bar line)

Write the F major pentatonic scale in the bass clef

Name these key signatures and write the tonic.

_____   _____   _____

Write these intervals above the written note

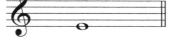

     Minor 2nd   Perfect 5th   Perfect 4th

Write a triad above each note.

Insert a time signature for this piece. What is the metre? _____

48

Theory - skills practice 4

Note review: Bass clef - write these notes using semibreves.

G   B   F   C   E   A   C   D

Write a major scale starting on the note provided. What scale is this? _____

Rewrite the same scale in the bass clef using a key signature.

Write the key signatures for the tonic provided.

Identify these intervals from the following options: minor 2nd, major 2nd, perfect 4th, perfect 5th, perfect 8ve

_____   _____   _____

Write these intervals above the written note

Perfect 8ve   Perfect 5th   Perfect 4th

Write a triad above each note.

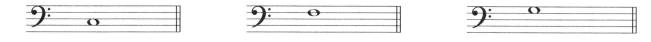

Rewrite these bars with the correct note grouping.

Theory - skills practice 5

Note review: Treble clef

_____

Write a major scale starting on the note provided. What scale is this? _____

Rewrite the same scale in the treble clef using acidentals instead of a key signature.

Name these key signatures and write the tonic.

_____   _____   _____

Write these intervals above the written note

Minor 2nd   Perfect 5th   Perfect 4th

Write a triad above each note.

Insert a time signature for this piece. What is the metre? _____

Theory - skills practice 6

Write a major scale starting on the note provided. What scale is this? _____

Rewrite the same scale in the bass clef using a key signature.

Identify the key and write the notes according to the scale degree name provided.

Key: _____

Tonic   Mediant   Dominant

Identify these intervals.

_____   _____   _____

Write the primary triads of C major in the treble clef. Remember the double bar line.

Rewrite these bars with the correct note grouping.

Theory - skills practice 7

Write a major pentatonic scale starting on G in the treble clef using semibreves.

Write a major pentatonic scale starting on F in the bass clef using semibreves.

Identify the key and write the notes according to the scale degree name provided.

Key: _____

Tonic   Subdominant   Submediant

Write these intervals above the written note

Perfect 8ve   Perfect 5th   Perfect 4th

Write the primary triads of G major in the treble clef. Remember the key signature in each bar.

Insert a time signature for this piece. What is the metre? _____

Theory - skills practice 8

Write the major scale with one sharp in the bass clef with a key signature.

Write the major scale with one flat in the treble clef with a key signature.

Identify the key and write the notes according to the scale degree name provided.

Key: _____

Leadingnote   Supertonic   Mediant

Name these intervals.

_____   _____   _____

Write the primary triads of F major in the treble clef.

Rewrite these bars with the correct note grouping.

Theory - skills practice 9

Write the scale as indicated by the key signature.

Write the scale as indicated by the key signature.

Identify the key and write the notes according to the scale degree name provided.

Key: _____

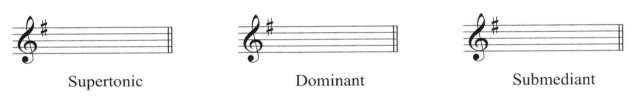

Supertonic   Dominant   Submediant

Write these intervals above the written note

Minor 2nd   Perfect 5th   Perfect 4th

Identify the key and write the primary triads.   Key: _____

Insert bar lines for this melody.

Theory - skills practice 10

Write the scale as indicated by the key signature.

Write the scale as indicated by the key signature.

Identify the key and write the notes according to the scale degree name provided.

Key: _____

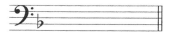      

Subdominant   Leading note   Tonic

Name these intervals.

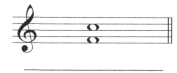   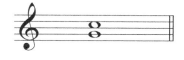   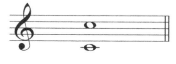

_____   _____   _____

Identify the key and write the primary triads.   Key: _____

Insert bar lines for this melody.

Section 4: Analysis

Italian Terms

Write the definition for each of these terms:

Largo _____

Adagio _____

Andante _____

Allegretto _____

Moderato _____

Allegro _____

Presto _____

Accelerando _____

Rallentando _____

Crescendo _____

Decrescendo _____

Legato _____

Staccato _____

Pianissimo _____

Piano _____

Mezzo Piano _____

Mezzo Forte _____

Forte _____

Fortissimo _____

Italian Terms

Write each of these terms in the correct column according to tempo, dynamics or style.

Largo, Allegretto, Adagio, Andante, Moderato, Allegro, Presto, Legato, Staccato, Accelerando, Rallentando, Crescendo, Decrescendo, Pianissimo, Piano, Mezzo Piano, Mezzo Forte, Forte, Fortissimo

Tempo	*Dynamics*	*Style*
_____	_____	_____
_____	_____	_____
_____	_____	_____
_____	_____	_____
_____	_____	_____
_____	_____	_____
_____	_____	_____
_____	_____	_____
_____	_____	_____
_____	_____	_____

Study the melody below and answer the following questions.

Andante

1. What is the key? _____

   Write the scale on the stave below in the treble clef.

2. Add dynamics to indicate that the piece starts soft and then becomes softer in the final bar.

3. What is the tempo? _____

4. Name the intervals as marked on the score.

   i) _____   ii) _____

Italian Terms

Define these terms relating to tempo:

Largo   _____

Adagio   _____

Moderato   _____

Allegro   _____

Presto   _____

Study the melody below and answer the following questions.

Allegro

1. What is the key? _____

   Write the scale on the stave below in the bass clef.

2. What is the tempo? _____

3. What is the metre? _____

4. Name the intervals as marked on the score.

   i) _____   ii) _____

Italian Terms

Define these terms relating to dynamics:

piano   _____

forte   _____

mezzo forte   _____

diminuendo   _____

pianissimo   _____

Study the melody below and answer the following questions.

Adagio

p

1. What is the key? _____

   Write the scale on the stave below in the treble clef.

2. What is the tempo? _____

3. What is the metre? _____

4. Name the intervals as marked on the score.

   i) _____   ii) _____

5. What is the dynamic marking? _____

Italian Terms

Write the Italian term for these definitions:

Broadly   _____

Leisurely   _____

Moderately   _____

Lively and fast   _____

Fast   _____

Study the melody below and answer the following questions.

Moderato

1. What is the key? _____

   Write the scale on the stave below in the treble clef.

2. What is the tempo? _____

3. What is the metre? _____

4. Name the intervals as marked on the score.

   i) _____   ii) _____

5. What is the dynamic marking? _____

Italian Terms

Define these terms:

Largo   _____

Adagio   _____

Allegro   _____

Presto   _____

Andante   _____

Study the melody below and answer the following questions.

Presto

1. What scale does this melody use? _____

   Write the scale on the stave below in the treble clef.

2. What is the tempo? _____

3. Define the dynamics used in this piece. _____

4. Name the intervals as marked on the score.

   i) _____   ii) _____

Italian Terms

Define these terms:

piano   _____

forte   _____

mezzo forte   _____

diminuendo   _____

pianissimo   _____

crescendo   _____

fortissimo   _____

Study the melody below and answer the following questions.

Largo

1. What scale does this melody use? _____

   Write the scale on the stave below in the bass clef.

2. What is the tempo? _____

3. What is the metre? _____

4. Define the dynamics used in this piece. _____

5. Name the intervals as marked on the score.

   i) _____   ii) _____

Italian Terms

Write the Italian term for these definitions:

Very Loud   _____

Very soft   _____

Loud   _____

Soft   _____

Moderately loud   _____

Moderately soft   _____

Getting softer   _____

Study the melody below and answer the following questions.

Andante

1. What is the key? _____

   Write the scale on the stave below in the treble clef.

2. Define the dynamics used in this piece. _____

3. What is the tempo? _____

4. What is the metre? _____

5. Name the intervals as marked on the score.

   i) _____   ii) _____

Italian Terms

Define these terms:

Largo   _____

Adagio   _____

Moderato   _____

Allegro   _____

Presto   _____

Piano   _____

Forte   _____

Study the melody below and answer the following questions.

Largo

1. What is the key? _____

   Write the scale on the stave below in the bass clef.

2. Define the dynamics used in this piece. _____

3. What is the tempo? _____

4. Name the intervals as marked on the score.

   i) _____   ii) _____

Italian Terms

Write the Italian term for these definitions:

Broadly _____

Leisurely _____

Moderately _____

Lively and fast _____

Fast _____

Getting faster _____

Study the melody below and answer the following questions.

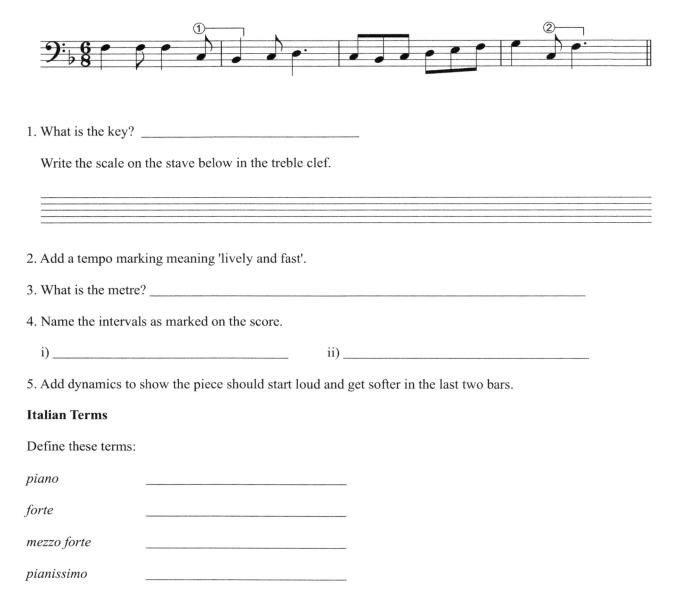

1. What is the key? _____

   Write the scale on the stave below in the treble clef.

2. Add a tempo marking meaning 'lively and fast'.

3. What is the metre? _____

4. Name the intervals as marked on the score.

   i) _____   ii) _____

5. Add dynamics to show the piece should start loud and get softer in the last two bars.

Italian Terms

Define these terms:

piano   _____

forte   _____

mezzo forte   _____

pianissimo   _____

crescendo   _____

fortissimo   _____

Study the melody below and answer the following questions.

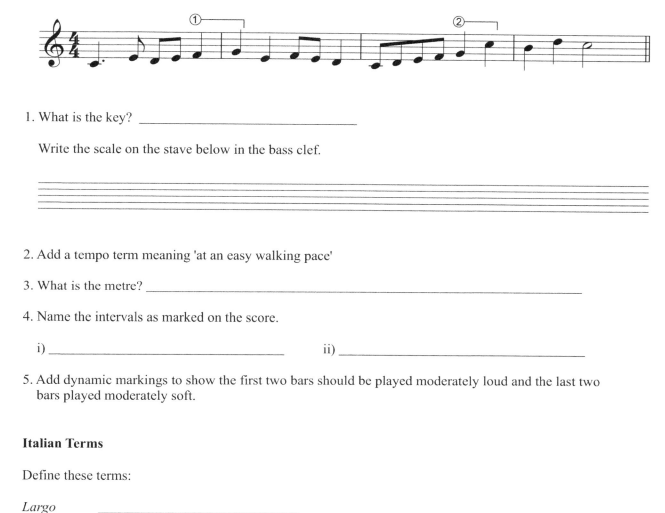

1. What is the key? _____

   Write the scale on the stave below in the bass clef.

2. Add a tempo term meaning 'at an easy walking pace'

3. What is the metre? _____

4. Name the intervals as marked on the score.

   i) _____   ii) _____

5. Add dynamic markings to show the first two bars should be played moderately loud and the last two bars played moderately soft.

Italian Terms

Define these terms:

Largo   _____

Adagio   _____

Moderato   _____

Andante   _____

Allegro   _____

Presto   _____

Accelerando   _____

Section 5: Working Space

94

Topic: _____   Date: _____

_____
_____
_____
_____
_____
_____
_____
_____
_____
_____
_____
_____
_____
_____
_____
_____
_____
_____
_____
_____
_____
_____
_____
_____
_____
_____
_____

Topic: _____   Date: _____

_____
_____
_____
_____
_____
_____
_____
_____
_____
_____
_____
_____
_____
_____
_____
_____
_____
_____
_____
_____
_____
_____
_____
_____
_____

Topic: _____   Date: _____

_____

_____

_____

_____

_____

_____

_____

_____

_____

_____

_____

_____

_____

_____

_____

_____

_____

_____

_____

_____

_____

_____

_____

_____

Topic: _____   Date: _____

_____

_____

_____

_____

_____

_____

_____

_____

_____

_____

_____

_____

_____

_____

_____

_____

_____

_____

_____

_____

_____

_____

_____

_____

_____

Topic: _____   Date: _____

Topic: _____   Date: _____

_____

_____

_____

_____

_____

_____

_____

_____

_____

_____

_____

_____

_____

_____

_____

_____

_____

_____

_____

_____

_____

_____

_____

Topic: _____   Date: _____

_____

_____

_____

_____

_____

_____

_____

_____

_____

_____

_____

_____

_____

_____

_____

_____

_____

_____

_____

_____

_____

_____

_____

_____

_____

_____

_____

_____

_____

Topic: _____   Date: _____

_____

_____

_____

_____

_____

_____

_____

_____

_____

_____

_____

_____

_____

_____

_____

_____

_____

_____

_____

_____

_____

_____

_____

_____

_____

_____

_____

Topic: _____   Date: _____

_____

_____

_____

_____

_____

_____

_____

_____

_____

_____

_____

_____

_____

_____

_____

_____

_____

_____

_____

_____

_____

_____

_____

Topic: _____   Date: _____

_____

_____

_____

_____

_____

_____

_____

_____

_____

_____

_____

_____

_____

_____

_____

_____

_____

_____

_____

_____

_____

_____

_____

Topic: _____   Date: _____

_____

_____

_____

_____

_____

_____

_____

_____

_____

_____

_____

_____

_____

_____

_____

_____

_____

_____

_____

_____

_____

_____

_____

_____

Topic: _____   Date: _____

_____

_____

_____

_____

_____

_____

_____

_____

_____

_____

_____

_____

_____

_____

_____

_____

_____

_____

_____

_____

_____

_____

_____

_____

_____

_____

Topic: _____   Date: _____

Topic: _____   Date: _____

_____
_____
_____
_____
_____
_____
_____
_____
_____
_____
_____
_____
_____
_____
_____
_____
_____
_____
_____
_____
_____
_____
_____
_____
_____
_____
_____

Topic: _____   Date: _____

_____
_____
_____
_____
_____
_____
_____
_____
_____
_____
_____
_____
_____
_____
_____
_____
_____
_____
_____
_____
_____
_____
_____
_____
_____
_____

Topic: _____   Date: _____

_____

_____

_____

_____

_____

_____

_____

_____

_____

_____

_____

_____

_____

_____

_____

_____

_____

_____

_____

_____

_____

_____

_____

_____

Topic: _____   Date: _____

_____

_____

_____

_____

_____

_____

_____

_____

_____

_____

_____

_____

_____

_____

_____

_____

_____

_____

_____

_____

_____

_____

_____

_____

_____

_____

Topic: _____   Date: _____

_____

_____

_____

_____

_____

_____

_____

_____

_____

_____

_____

_____

_____

_____

_____

_____

_____

_____

_____

_____

_____

_____

_____

_____

_____

_____

Topic: _____   Date: _____

_____

_____

_____

_____

_____

_____

_____

_____

_____

_____

_____

_____

_____

_____

_____

_____

_____

_____

_____

_____

_____

_____

_____

_____

_____

Topic: _____   Date: _____

_____
_____
_____
_____
_____
_____
_____
_____
_____
_____
_____
_____
_____
_____
_____
_____
_____
_____
_____
_____
_____
_____
_____
_____
_____
_____

Topic: _____   Date: _____

_____

_____

_____

_____

_____

_____

_____

_____

_____

_____

_____

_____

_____

_____

_____

_____

_____

_____

_____

_____

_____

_____

_____

_____

_____

_____

_____

_____

_____

Topic: _____   Date: _____

_____
_____
_____
_____
_____
_____
_____
_____
_____
_____
_____
_____
_____
_____
_____
_____
_____
_____
_____
_____
_____
_____
_____
_____

Topic: _____   Date: _____

About the Author

Sarah Stopher completed a Bachelor of Music Education at the University of Western Australia in 2004. Since then, she has worked in a country town in the North West of Australia for three years before relocating to Perth. The Aural Development Program was developed to provide her students with the opportunity to develop their aural skills at their own pace. The first book was used with a group of Year 10 students in 2010 and proved a great success, particularly with students with little or no aural training.